FAITH AND HEALTH DEVOTIONAL SERIES

REBUILD YOUR TEMPLE
GOD'S WAY®

BOOK 1: RESTORE YOUR BODY

A 10-DAY JOURNEY TO
PHYSICAL HEALTH AND WHOLENESS

STEPHANIE L. FRANKLIN-SUBER

Dedication

To my adored husband, **Berchard V. Suber**, and my son, **Michael Franklin Suber**—for your unwavering love, prayers, and sacrifices throughout my nearly twenty-year journey to reclaim a life of healing and wholeness.

Through cancer, chronic illness, and cardiac arrest, you stood beside me with faith and courage. You have been living reminders that love endures all things and that God's grace truly sustains.

To **Reverend Anna Grant-Borden** and to the members of **Mount Airy Presbyterian Church**, past, present, and future.

To every woman embarking on the journey of healing and wholeness— may you discover the beauty of Rebuilding Your Temple, God's Way®.

With profound gratitude to my **Heavenly Father**, my Creator, whose healing power knows no limit and whose grace restores body, soul, and spirit.

May You be glorified.

Blessed by the support of Cathy Morenzie, Preston Squire, and Jennifer Eastmond, and by the gifted work of Alec Gerhart and Rachel Aponte.

Foreword

Do you not know that your body is a temple of the Holy Spirit who is within you, whom you have from God, and that you are not your own? You were bought with a price [you were actually purchased with the precious blood of Jesus and made His own]. So then, honor and glorify God with your body.
(1 Corinthians 6:19–20 AMP)

Our bodies are sacred edifices, masterfully created by God for His glory and for worship. In Psalm 19:1, King David declares, *"The heavens declare the glory of God; the skies proclaim the work of his hands."* Just as the heavens reflect the majesty of God, so do we — His beloved creation. We are the workmanship of His hands, *"fearfully and wonderfully made."*

Yet as we journey through life, the demands placed on our bodies — some self-imposed and others thrust upon us by circumstances, people, or illness — can leave us depleted, wounded, or disconnected from the God who created us. In these moments of weariness and brokenness, we stand in need of **restoration**, **renewal**, and **realignment** with our Creator.

In this beautifully architected and God-inspired devotional collection, Stephanie Franklin-Suber gently but powerfully guides you through a sacred journey to restore your body, renew your soul, and realign your spirit.

Stephanie has walked this very path — from brokenness into wholeness through the transformative power of God's Word. God miraculously healed and delivered her from cancer, from years of chronic illness, and most recently from cardiac arrest. In each chapter of her testimony, God revealed to her the sacredness of her temple and showed her that, through faith in Jesus Christ, through Scripture, and by the work of the Holy Spirit, her temple could be rebuilt — God's way. Today, God has called Stephanie to help others rebuild their temples: body, soul, and spirit.

It is with joy and deep gratitude that I introduce you to this ***Rebuild Your Temple, God's Way® Signature Faith and Health Collection***, which includes the three-book *10-Day Devotional Series* (*Restore Your Body, Renew Your Soul*, and *Realign Your Spirit*) and the two-book *30-Day Devotional Series* (the *30-Day Devotional* and the companion *Bible Study Workbook*).

As you embark on this sacred journey, do so with **anticipation** and **expectation**. Allow the Word of God to minister to your soul through Scripture and Reflection. Worship God with your body through the daily Temple

Practice. Receive God's healing and restoration by engaging the Health Coaching Tips. And experience spiritual alignment as your spirit connects with the Spirit of God through prayer and journaling in the *Rebuild Your Temple, God's Way® Journal.*

It is my honor and delight to invite you to experience this transformational journey.

Come, and Rebuild Your Temple, God's Way®.

Yours in Christ,
Rev. Anna L. Grant-Borden
Senior Pastor, Mt. Airy Presbyterian Church
Philadelphia, Pennsylvania

Table of Contents

Daily Devotionals
Each day includes Scripture, Reflection, Temple Practice, Health Coaching Tip, Prayer, Journal Prompt, and Affirmation.

You are encouraged to use the Rebuild Your Temple, God's Way® Journal or your own personal journal to capture your prayers, insights, and reflections each day.

Author's Introduction

Your body is one of God's greatest gifts—a sacred Triune Human Temple™ (Body–Soul–Spirit) where His Spirit dwells. When God gave King David the design for the Holy Temple in Jerusalem, it reflected His own triune nature: Father, Son, and Holy Spirit. The Temple had three parts—the *Outer Court*, the *Inner Court*, and the *Holiest of Holies*—each representing a deeper place of worship and intimacy with Him.

You, too, were created in God's triune image as a Triune Human Temple™ (Body–Soul–Spirit). Your **body** represents the *Outer Court*, where visible acts of worship and sacrifice take place. The **soul**—your mind, will, and emotions—mirrors the *Inner Court*, where thoughts and desires are consecrated to Him. And your **spirit** reflects the *Holiest of Holies*, where intimate communion with God occurs.

This devotional, *Restore Your Body*, begins your Triune Temple Journey™ in the *Outer Court*—your physical health. It is here, through daily acts of stewardship, that you prepare your temple for deeper renewal and realignment. Each choice to nourish, rest, or move with intention becomes an offering of praise, a small act of obedience that invites the presence of God the Father more fully into your life.

The pages that follow were born from my own journey of rebuilding my temple, God's way. Through cancer, chronic illness, and even cardiac arrest, my body was broken again and again—but each time, God faithfully healed and restored it. What He did for me; He can do for you. Restoration is not about perfection; it is about partnership with the One who heals, strengthens, and dwells in you.

Over the next ten days, you will be guided through Scripture, reflection, and simple practices that help you rebuild the outer court of your temple. You honor God the Father by honoring your body.

Each day includes:

- **Scripture** to anchor your journey in the unfailing Word of your Creator,
- **Reflection** to learn how and why our Heavenly Father cares about your physical health,
- **Temple Practice** to help you put stewardship of your health into action,
- **Health Coaching Tip** to apply His wisdom in your daily health choices,

- **Prayer** to draw on His love and strength to sustain you,

- **Journal Prompt** to record your insights and progress, and

- **Affirmation** to encourage and motivate you throughout your day.

Together, these practices will help you slow down, listen to your body, and rediscover the sacred rhythm of rest, nourishment, and renewal. As you restore your body, may you also draw closer to the God who created it, designed it, and desires to dwell within it.

God the Father invites you to begin this journey to restore your body— His way.

 DAY 1 – YOUR BODY IS A TEMPLE

Scripture
Do you not know that your bodies are temples of the Holy Spirit, who is in you, whom you have received from God? You are not your own; you were bought at a price. Therefore honor God with your bodies.
(1 Corinthians 6:19–20 NIV)

Reflection
Paul wrote these words to believers in Corinth, a culture that treated the body as something to indulge or ignore. He reminded them that redemption makes the body sacred—it now belongs to the Lord who purchased it.

Your body, like the *Outer Court* of God's Temple, is where your daily worship begins. Caring for your physical health is not vanity; it is stewardship. Each nourishing choice, each moment of rest, each step taken in gratitude becomes a form of worship that honors the God who dwells within you. When you view your body as His dwelling, self-care transforms from duty to devotion.

Today, invite your Creator to show you one area—nutrition, hydration, movement, breathing, or rest—where He wants to restore reverence.

Temple Practice
Choose one gentle action today that blesses your body—walk, stretch, breathe, sip water slowly, or rest intentionally—and thank God with each choice and action.

Health Coaching Tip
Start with small, simple steps to honor your body as God's entrusted gift. Consistency matters more than intensity. Faithful repetition transforms simple acts into lasting habits of stewardship and care.

Prayer
Heavenly Father,
Thank You for creating my body as Your temple. Teach me to honor You through how I care for it today.
In Jesus' name, I pray, Amen.

Journal Prompt
What would change if you treated your body as a sacred space of worship?

Affirmation
I honor God by honoring my temple through every choice I make.

 DAY 2 – NOURISH YOUR TEMPLE

Scripture
So whether you eat or drink or whatever you do, do it all for the glory of God.
(1 Corinthians 10:31 NIV)

Reflection
From the manna in the wilderness to the loaves and fishes that fed the multitude, Scripture shows God's concern for daily bread. Every meal is His reminder that He provides what sustains both body and soul. When you eat with gratitude, ordinary nourishment becomes sacred fellowship.

Paul's instruction to the Corinthians calls you to shift your focus from self to glory: eating and drinking become opportunities to magnify the Giver.

Invite God to the table. Slow your pace; notice texture, color, and flavor; receive each bite as grace. Healthy eating is not restriction—it is agreement with the Lord's desire for your flourishing.

Temple Practice
Pause before eating today. Pray a short blessing and take your first three bites slowly, thanking God for flavor, texture, and strength.

Health Coaching Tip
Plan balanced meals with lean protein, colorful produce, and whole grains. Mindful eating improves digestion and satisfaction.

Prayer
Heavenly Father,
Thank You for the gift of food that nourishes my body and reflects Your goodness. Help me to eat with mindfulness and gratitude.
In Jesus' name, I pray, Amen.

Journal Prompt
How can mealtime become an act of worship in your daily rhythm?

Affirmation
I take every bite with gratitude to honor the God who sustains me.

DAY 3 – HYDRATE AND REFRESH

Scripture
The Lord will guide you always; He will satisfy your needs in a sun-scorched land and will strengthen your frame. You will be like a well-watered garden, like a spring whose waters never fail.
(Isaiah 58:11 NIV)

Reflection
In Isaiah's promise to a weary people, God likens His care to water flowing through dry ground. Just as the earth thirsts for rain, our bodies long for refreshment. Water is one of the simplest yet most profound reminders of His provision—it cleanses, cools, and sustains every system He designed.

When you pause to drink, remember the Living Water who never fails. Hydration becomes worship when it turns your thoughts toward dependence on Him. Let each sip remind you that He strengthens your frame and refreshes your purpose.

Temple Practice
Drink a full glass of water before each meal today, thanking God for the refreshment of His presence.

Health Coaching Tip
Aim for eight cups of water daily. Keep a refillable bottle nearby, and infuse with fruit or herbs for variety.

Prayer
Heavenly Father,
Please refresh my body. Quench my thirst with Your provision and renew my strength for the work ahead.
In Jesus' name, I pray, Amen.

Journal Prompt
How does physical refreshment remind you of God's continual renewal?

Affirmation
I am refreshed by the Living Water and strengthened to flourish.

 DAY 4 – MOVE WITH GRACE

Scripture
For in Him we live and move and have our being.
(Acts 17:28 NIV)

Reflection
Paul's declaration in Athens grounds all movement in divine origin. Every heartbeat and step are evidence of God's sustaining power. He designed motion not just for function, but for joy.

When you move your body, you participate in His creative rhythm.

In the *Outer Court* of the Temple in Jerusalem, priests served through continual motion—lifting, carrying, preparing offerings. Their labor was worship. Your daily movement can carry the same intention. Whether you stretch, walk, or exercise, do it as prayer in motion. Graceful movement honors the One who gives breath and energy, reminding you that strength and coordination are gifts to steward, not possessions to boast in.

Temple Practice
Take a brisk walk or gentle stretch while thanking God for the ability to move and serve Him.

Health Coaching Tip
Consistent movement improves circulation, joint health, and mood. Find activities you enjoy—walking, dancing, gardening—to keep it sustainable.

Prayer
Creator God,
Thank You for the gift of movement. Help me to use my strength to praise and serve You with joy and grace.
In Jesus' name, I pray, Amen.

Journal Prompt
How can you turn everyday movement into worship?

Affirmation
I live, move, and have my being in God, and my motion is worship.

 DAY 5 – BREATHE AND RELEASE

Scripture
Then the Lord God formed a man from the dust of the ground and breathed into his nostrils the breath of life, and the man became a living being.
(Genesis 2:7 NIV)

Reflection
Life began with God's breath. That same divine rhythm continues in you—inhale grace, exhale surrender. Each breath is both miracle and message: you live because He gives. When anxiety constricts your breathing, remember that peace is only one deep inhale away.

The Hebrew word for "breath," *ruach,* also means "spirit." Breathing slowly and intentionally reconnects you with the One who animates your being. In those moments, stress yields to presence, and fear gives way to faith. Let today's breathing become a holy conversation—receiving His Spirit, releasing your burdens.

Temple Practice
Pause three times today to take five slow, deep breaths. Inhale God's peace; exhale every care.

Health Coaching Tip
Deep breathing lowers stress hormones and steadies heart rate. Practice before meals or bedtime for calm and clarity.

Prayer
Creator God,
I praise You for breathing Your life into my body. Help me to calm my nervous system by releasing tension so that I can rest in Your presence.
In Jesus' name, I pray, Amen.

Journal Prompt
What do you need to exhale and surrender to God today?

Affirmation
I receive God's peace and release my burdens with each breath I take.

 DAY 6 – BE STILL AND KNOW HIM

Scripture
Be still, and know that I am God; I will be exalted among the nations, I will be exalted in the earth.
(Psalm 46:10 NIV)

Reflection
The psalmist wrote these words in the middle of chaos—nations raging, mountains trembling, waters roaring. God's command was not for inactivity but for trust: *Be still.* In stillness, you remember that the world turns by His hand, not yours. Stress and anxiety often drive you to over-function; quietness recenters you on the sufficiency of God the Father.

When you practice stillness, you enter the inner sanctuary of peace even while tending to your outer-court body. A few minutes of silence can reset your heartbeat and renew your mind. It is in the quiet that you hear His gentle whisper reminding you, "I am God, and I am with you."

Temple Practice
Sit in silence today for five minutes. Focus on slow breathing and repeat, "You are God, and I trust You."

Health Coaching Tip
Intentional quiet lowers blood pressure and cortisol. Unplug from screens daily and let your body experience calm.

Prayer
Almighty God,
Teach me to be still in Your presence. Under the shadow of Your wings, I am safe and protected. Quiet my racing thoughts so I may know You more deeply.
In Jesus' name, I pray, Amen.

Journal Prompt
What distractions keep you from being still before God?

Affirmation
I find God's strength and peace in stillness.

 DAY 7 – REST TO REBUILD

Scripture
In vain you rise early and stay up late, toiling for food to eat—for He grants sleep to those He loves.
(Psalm 127:2 NIV)

Reflection
The builder who never sleeps eventually weakens his foundation. God created night and day so that work and rest would partner together. Sleep is not wasted time—it is sacred rebuilding.

While you rest, God repairs tissues, restores hormones, and renews energy for purpose. The body you steward needs this rhythm to thrive.

Israel's farmers practiced Sabbath rest to trust God with provision; your nightly rest is a smaller Sabbath of faith. When you lie down, you declare that God is working even when you are not.

Let each evening become an altar where you lay down your labor and receive His rest. As your body regains strength, may it serve as a vessel for God's good work.

Temple Practice
Turn off electronics 30 minutes before bed. Dim the lights, breathe deeply, and thank God for His faithful protection while you sleep.

Health Coaching Tip
Aim for 7–8 hours of sleep. A dark, cool room and a consistent bedtime support hormone balance and recovery.

Prayer
Most High God,
Thank You for rest that restores. Help me to trust that You are working all things together for my good and that You are healing and restoring my body all through the night.
In Jesus' name, I pray, Amen.

Journal Prompt
How does trusting God change the way you approach sleep and rest?

Affirmation
I receive God's gift of rest and awake restored.

 # DAY 8 – LISTEN TO YOUR BODY

Scripture
Then he lay down under the bush and fell asleep. All at once an angel touched him and said, "Get up and eat." He looked around, and there by his head was some bread baked over hot coals, and a jar of water.
(1 Kings 19:5–6 NIV)

Reflection
After Elijah's great victory came exhaustion and despair. God's response was practical: sleep, food, and water. The Lord cared for Elijah's physical needs before speaking to his heart. In the same way, your body's signals—fatigue, hunger, tension—are invitations from God to slow down and receive care. Listening is holy stewardship.

When you ignore your body, you silence one of God's messengers. When you respond with compassion, you align with His design. God does not condemn your limitations; He meets you in them.

Temple Practice
Check in with your body three times today. Ask, "What do I need right now—rest, nourishment, or movement?"

Health Coaching Tip
Regular body awareness prevents burnout. Gentle stretching, hydration, and balanced meals keep energy steady.

Prayer
Lord of Lords,
Thank You for creating my body with wisdom. Help me listen and respond with kindness and gratitude.
In Jesus' name, I pray, Amen.

Journal Prompt
What message is your body sending you today, and how will you respond?

Affirmation
I am fearfully and wonderfully made; I listen to my body with grace.

 DAY 9 – RENEW YOUR STRENGTH

Scripture
But those who hope in the Lord will renew their strength. They will soar on wings like eagles; they will run and not grow weary, they will walk and not be faint.
(Isaiah 40:31 NIV)

Reflection
Isaiah spoke to a weary nation in exile, reminding them that hope—not human effort—renews strength. God promises endurance for those who wait on Him. Physical strength mirrors spiritual truth: energy flows from the Source.

When you nourish your body, hydrate, and move, you participate in the renewal He provides. Stewardship of health prepares you for Kingdom purpose. Renewal happens when you exchange exhaustion for empowerment. Waiting on God is not idle—it is aligning your rhythms with His.

As you care for your body, He multiplies your stamina to serve.

Temple Practice
Take a short walk or do a gentle stretch while praying Isaiah 40:31. Feel His promise strengthening your steps.

Health Coaching Tip
Balanced meals, hydration, and consistent movement maintain energy. Ten minutes outdoors can reset body and mind.

Prayer
Father,
Thank You for renewing my strength. Help me to wait patiently as You heal my body. Teach me to care for my body with wisdom and gratitude.
In Jesus' name, I pray, Amen.

Journal Prompt
Where do you need to exchange weariness for God's renewing strength?

Affirmation
I wait on the Lord, and He renews my strength daily for His purpose.

 DAY 10 – CELEBRATE YOUR PROGRESS

Scripture
Being confident of this, that He who began a good work in you will carry it on to completion until the day of Christ Jesus.
(Philippians 1:6 NIV)

Reflection
Your faith and health journey is one of progress, not perfection. Paul's words remind you that God Himself is the finisher of the work He begins. Each small change—one more glass of water, one mindful meal, one restful night—is evidence of His grace in action. Celebrate your progress because celebration fuels perseverance. Gratitude shifts your focus from what remains undone to what God has already restored.

When you rejoice in every small step, you acknowledge that stewardship of your health is a journey of partnership with Him. The One who created you and began your healing will carry it to completion in His perfect timing.

Temple Practice
Write down three areas of progress from these ten days. Thank God for His faithfulness in each.

Health Coaching Tip
Celebrate wins with non-food rewards—time outdoors, music, or a relaxing bath—to reinforce healthy patterns.

Prayer
Lord,
I am grateful to You for the good work You have begun in me. Teach me to celebrate progress and trust Your process.
In Jesus' name, I pray, Amen.

Journal Prompt
How will you continue to celebrate and sustain your progress with God?

Affirmation
I rejoice in every step God helps me take toward health and wholeness.

# Closing Prayer – Restore Your Body

Heavenly Father,

Thank You for meeting me in this sacred journey of restoration.
You have reminded me that my body is Your temple—a vessel of worship, not of striving; a dwelling of grace, not of guilt.

As I continue to rebuild my temple, teach me to see every healthy choice as an act of faith. May nourishment, rest, and movement become offerings of love to You. Please continue to guide my steps, breathe Your breath of life into my lungs, and strengthen my hands for the restoration work You have called me to do.

Thank You for healing what was physically broken and restoring what seemed beyond repair. Help me walk in courage and confidence, knowing that You who began this good work in me will carry it to completion.

I dedicate this restored body—Your temple—back to You, for Your service, Your glory, and Your purpose.

In Jesus' name, I pray, Amen.

Continue Your Triune Temple Journey™

Congratulations!

You have completed *Book 1 – Restore Your Body: A 10-Day Journey to Physical Health and Wholeness* in the *Rebuild Your Temple, God's Way® Faith and Health 10-Day Devotional Series*.

During this first stage of your Triune Temple Journey™, you have learned to honor your body as God's dwelling place—to nourish it with gratitude, rest it with trust, move it with grace, and breathe in His presence daily.

But this is just the beginning...

Just as the Temple in Jerusalem had deeper courts leading toward God's presence, your journey continues inward—from body to soul to spirit.

Continue your Triune Temple Journey™ with:

🕯️ *Book 2 – Renew Your Soul: A 10-Day Journey to Emotional Health and Mindset Renewal*

💜 *Book 3 – Realign Your Spirit: A 10-Day Journey to Spiritual Health and Wholeness*

Visit www.rebuildyourtemplegodsway.com to explore transformational Christian health coaching programs and resources designed to help you reclaim and maintain a life of health and wholeness—body, soul, and spirit—God's way.

Restore Your Body. Renew Your Soul. Realign Your Spirit.™

www.ingramcontent.com/pod-product-compliance
Lightning Source LLC
Chambersburg PA
CBHW040906120626
46551CB00006B/671